NEWER KID DICTIONARY

Quotes from children and adults
in the course of Parenting

LAZAR SARNA

Inquiries and Book Orders should be addressed to:

Great Writers Media
Email: info@greatwritersmedia.com
Phone: 877-600-5469

ISBN: 978-1-960939-44-9 (sc)
ISBN: 978-1-960939-45-6 (ebk)

INTRODUCTION

The *Newer Kid Dictionary* is a compilation of original expressions, queries, explanations and utterances, (all off-the-cuff) by kids and adults faced with usually common or surprising circumstances. These have been captured and set down here in their original form, thereby preserving the humour, innocence, joy and curiosity that language can offer.

Sometimes the wording may be twisted or incomplete. Often the idea is there but half-baked in its expression. These sayings capture a stage in life and a snap-shot of a moment frozen forever in this book.

The contents are not meant to make fun of anyone: on the contrary they glorify the creativity and courage of expression. They summarize in a way the path travelled by two of the Offers (Authors) during their fifty years of marriage.

PART ONE:

CONVERSATIONS

A

AGE

As I get older, I just replace hope with Advil.

_____

Michelle Franklin coping

I've decided not to age any further.

_____

Elaine Lazarus on the wisest approach.

They don't write enough songs about shopping.

_____

Michi lamenting an unsung Old Navy Store.

Good thing people age when they're old. Young people couldn't handle it.

_____

Efraim considering the lot of mankind.

And so the horror show begins.

_____

Jewel noticing how old friends have aged.

I want to retire from elementary school.

_____

Nava planning her future.

ANIMALS

He barks every morning at 6 o'clock.

He thinks he's a rooster.

Jewel, describing the neighbour's dog.

I like dogs.....with no teeth.

Uncle Aaron, lamenting the rarity of such canines.

Horse-fish.

Tova, trying to translate the Hebrew word for sea-horse.

The dog's bark is bigger than himself.

Lazar making an interesting comparison

I think black rabbits are poisonous. All animals with red eyes are poisonous. Snakes hide their poisonous identity, even though they don't have red eyes. For example, tarantulas are poisonous and don't have red eyes.

Levi with amazing biological insight.

My favourite animal is a unicorn because it is so colourful and pretty.

T.T. the vet.

ANOMALIES

I'm hot. I need earmuffs made of ice.
Ice muffs.

Dov, reacting to the temperature.

This marshmallow is good even after Tat stepped on it.

———————————————

Michi, savouring a surprisingly good snack.

If no-one wants the gefilte fish juice, I'm going to drink all of it myself.

———————————————

Jewel, never wanting to let good food go to waste.

-Everyone has a cell phone. Why can't I have one?
-*Tat doesn't have one.*
-......(Quizzical silence)

———————————————

Eitan, trying to convince his mother.

ANSWERING MACHINE

I'm only accepting messages from wrong numbers.

Please leave a message *before* the beep.

Hello, I'm not here, I'm elsewhere. Where else?

Please leave a message unless you're uni-neuronal.

Please leave a message in sign language or Morse-code.

Please leave a message if you're carbon-based.

Please leave a message while yodeling.

Please leave a message in hieroglyphics.

Hi, this is the guy you're calling. Please leave a message.

Dov's recorded messages on his answering machine.

APPETITE

Time for lunch.

Levi immediately upon hearing church bells

You made me hiccup!

Levi protesting.

It's like you're the teeth and I'm the gum.

Levi being embraced by his mother

They should make tables longer.
Why?
My food keeps falling on the floor between me and the end of the table.
You mean you need a plastic bib to catch your food.

Tat complaining about inadequate furniture.

I hope you are hungry.
There's always room for food.

Jewel and Csaba awkwardly responding to the hostess of an elaborate meal after forgetting about the invitation, and after having finished eating voraciously at a restaurant just minutes before.

ATHLETICS

I'm ok. I broke my fall with my head.

Lazar explaining his bicycle prowess.

ATMOSPHERE

It's still light outside. I'm going to sleep wrong.

Racheli, negotiating with her parents to let her stay up later.

Why does my car always smell like a falafel stand?

Tova, taking a deep breath.

It looks like the emergency ward at the hospital.

Jewel, walking into a crowded restaurant

-Why do you close the door?
-*I want my primacy.*

Ezra, talking bathroom etiquette with Avi.

Don't go there. You'll come back pregnant.

Marie-Josee Weigensberg recalling her trip to Israel.

Tat's bathroom smells like strawberries.

_____

Hillel's observation.

B

BEAUTY

Don't eat near my head. I'm going to sell my hair.

_____

Teenage Naomi.

You're cute.
-No, I'm beautiful

_____

Tehila, responding to a compliment

I'm getting to the age when my legs feel old.

_____

Adult Naomi chasing her kids.

Do you have a neck?
-Ella Weigensberg, looking at people's heads.

There's no such thing as Flemish.

_____

Michi, upon hearing what they speak in Belgium.

You are the cutest girl I ever met-ted.

_____

Daveed to Racheli.

My beard felt like a living pet on my face.

_____

Jessy, after shaving his summer growth.

I don't like your shirt. I don't like your skirt.....and I don't like your skin.

_____

Nava, sizing up Jewel's attire.

It's a work of art. We don't poke a hole in it with our finger.

_____

Naomi to Nava, over a painting.

That's your curb appeal.

_____

Tat to Jewel after she mis-stepped down from the sidewalk.

Your hair is too big for your head

_____

Nava observing her mother

You're looking very tall today.
That's because I am just very tall.

_____

Jewel conversing with Naomi

BIRTHDAY

I'm getting too old for my life.

_____

Fran Avni, thinking happy, thinking sad.

He's too young to be old.

Jewel, about someone she knows.

BOTANIST

What do I do with the watermelon crust?

Batya, after finishing her meal.

Feel this. Even the rocks are fresh.

Nava, examining a decorative stone in a hotel garden.

BOYS

They consider it a major personal achievement to wear socks for three consecutive days without their mother noticing.

They do not like to waste playtime by going to the bathroom.

They can't wait for their baby teeth to fall out even though they've just grown in.

They don't understand why kids can't drive big-people cars if they promise to be careful.

Tova, enumerating the basic factoids about little boys.

I fell down and hurt my Elmo.

Ami, nursing his arm.

Men don't have nipples. They have muscles.

Eitan, pounding his chest and then exclaiming, 'Ouch'.

Nava pee-ed on my skin, and that's not appropriate.

Levi complaining to Naomi

BUSINESS

Open until closing time.

Gerald, recalling sign in Switzerland.

I have a theory that kids get together once a week for a board meeting. They get out their agendas to schedule when each one is going to have a tantrum, so they don't overlap.

Tova, on why it is that kids never have simultaneous melt-downs.

I wouldn't get a haircut here. There's an axe in the window.

Jewel, looking at a barber shop in a small-town in upstate New York.

-This cookie has 6 grams of fat.
-_Is that with tax?_

Nava, asking older brother, Eitan, who knows more about accounting.

BUSY

We'll have to set you up with some play-dates when I'm studying.

Naomi to husband, Jessy, when he was aimlessly looking for something to do.

C

CHILDREN

Mamma, I'll take care of you, but only because I love you.
_____

Nava affectionately to her mother in the early morning

He was a good egg.
_____

Levi, mournfully, after accidentally dropping an egg on the floor.

How do you make chocolate chip cookies?
You take the chips and remove their toes so that they don't run away. Then you add them to the batter.
_____

Avi, explaining the recipe.

The only thing that will warm me up is summer.
Please turn on the hot air conditioners to warm up the car.
_____

Levi, riding in the car on a cold winter day.

Naomi to Nava, who is fighting with Levi: Don't use your hands, please use your words.
Nava: OK mama……(screaming) Levi, you're so stupid.
_____

A family brawl

Lazar: What's it like outside, Jewel?

Jewel: Quiet.

Lazar: Quiet is not a temperature.

Jewel as Lazar's weather forecaster.

Your food doesn't look good, but it tastes very delicious!

Eitan, the epicure, to his grandmother, Jewel.

Naomi to her three children who don't like what she brought for their picnic lunch: Look around you. Those other kids in the park aren't complaining. They're sitting quietly and eating their lunch.

Nava: That's because they didn't have to go through what you put us through.

Nava, giving her off-hand analysis of her childhood.

The older I get, the wiser my parents seem to be.

Dov, coming to a pivotal moment.

Tat invited us out for supper.
He said, "Let's go somewhere fancy.....like Cavendish Mall."

Naomi to Jewel, discussing Tat's initiative

CLARITY

For some reason, I've always confused celery with cucumbers.

Ezra, describing his inability to articulate concepts.

For some reason, I think in Celcius when it's cold and Fahrenheit when it's hot.

Ezra the weatherman.

He's talking baby-Chinese. He wants gum (so do I).

Daveed, explaining the babble of his brother, Ami.

I have a problem: I forget I am old.

Auntie Marlene Kon.

-Who was Confucius?
-He was a philosopher.
-So, he used to research fossils?

Nava, to story-telling Naomi.

CLEAN

I have a laundry in the oven.

Jewel, thinking about the washing machine.

I have a bump behind my ear.
-Come here, I have medicine.
No. I don't want you to put spit on my neck.

Batya, avoiding treatment by Tat.

CLOTHING

I *love* your accessories.

_____

Karlie Kloss, pointing to paper stickers that Ami stuck on Jewel's sweater.

Ouch! Get rid of it. It's hurting my eyes.

_____

Peggi (Cohen), viewing Jewel's dress as she models it.

CONSEQUENCES

Is it legal to take these evergreen branches to use as schach?
The neighbour put them out to get rid of them.

But his car is right next to the branches as well.
If we get caught, I get disbarred, but you go to jail.

_____

Csaba and Tat picking up cut foliage at the edge of a neighbour's lawn.

I heard of a scribe writing a mezuzah while travelling on a municipal bus.

And driving it at the same time?

_____

Ezra describing to Tat his new project of supervising standards.

CONSUMER

All I really need is more.

_____

Dov, on inconspicuous consumption.

-I went to Canadian Tire (hardware store).
-*Did you get me a generator?*

_____

Dov asking Jewel about her purchases.

COOKING

You get an etrog by putting a lemon in the microwave.

_____

Avi Segal, explaining the origins of a citrus fruit.

-The apple juice jar says 'made from concentrate'.
-*From concrete?*

_____

Mayaan, asking Jewel about nutrition.

CORRESPONDENCE

Dear Mom and Dad, I have some good news and some bad news.
The good news is I'm not making up the bad news.

_____

Little Moshe (Segal), writing home from camp.

COVID-19

Is today the last day of the curfew?
Let's take a picture of it.

_____

Lazar, wanting to preserve the moment for posterity.

Covid suits him.

_____

Moishe about his father who is known to enjoy staying at home and being by himself.

Covid isn't so popular anymore.

Avi the epidemiologist.

CREATIVE

Where do we keep the shovels? I want to build a moat in the back yard.

Michi, getting ready for a grand project.

When I was a little girl, I had Barbie dolls with no hair and a Ken doll with one leg.

Naomi, discussing her deprived childhood with Tova.

That was not a cough. It was a comment.

Tat, in denial

It's fictionary.

Talia to Tova, discussing a story.

They said I was a voracious reader.

Jewel, commenting on why the library committee needs her to stay on as a member.

CURE

Ima, I picked this flower for you so you won't be cranky.

_____

Yonatan, in the park.

You'll be his grand-dentist.

_____

Naomi, to her childhood dentist upon introducing him to her son, Eitan.

I'll get the vomitter.

_____

Eitan, responding to Naomi's diagnosis of fever.

-Mum had surgery to put a battery in her chest with electric wires that go to her heart. (pacemaker)
–So...now Mum's..... a robot?

_____

Eitan, reacting to Naomi's news about Jewel.

-Soon all your baby teeth will fall out and you'll grow adult teeth.
–And later all your grown up teeth fall out and you get grandma teeth.
-What are grandma teeth?
–Yellow and crooked.

_____

Naomi, discussing dental development with Nava.

D

DESIRE

I could eat that truck.

_____

Jewel, observing a truck painted with pictures of fruits and vegetables drive by.

I could fly like a butterfly but I only have toes.

Hannah, explaining herself.

As soon as we get home, let's drive to the forest.

Jewel, during a long drive from Toronto.

DIAGNOSIS

My lips are allergic to my spit.

Mayaan, commenting on her chapped lips.

Yehuda, good thing the doctors told me to wait three years before conceiving again. Otherwise, you would have been Naomi.

Jewel, speculating on birth order.

I'm a pain in my own neck.

Jewel, turning her face to the left.

DIPLOMACY

The best way to insult a Frenchman is to tell him:
Monsieur, your moustache is crooked.

Michi, quoting a friend who is in the know.

DISASTER

And the people were so bad that G-d sent down a giant marble on them.

Noah, after learning in nursery school about the Biblical Flood [mabul].

DISCRIMINATING

Even if I were secular, I wouldn't sleep with a man who was uncircumcised.

Name withheld for good reason.

He's a nice guy, but he wears two masks on his arm.

Dov, summing up Csaba.

I have no patience for impatient drivers.

Michi the on the rules of the road

E

EATING

I don't know it by heart. I need my denture.

Batya, trying to say Grace after meals without the text (bencher).

A vegetarian is a doctor for people who don't eat meat.

Avi, with medical insight.

Years ago when I was young, I was tall and slim. Now I'm tall.

_____

Tova, recounting the ravages of age.

Whenever you go to the supermarket, instead of buying food, you come home with chocolate or cinnamon danish.

_____

Jewel, with shopping insight for Lazar.

-It's supper time. Are you eating supper?
-*No, we're eating chips...... I don't know why.*

_____

Eitan, uncertain about his pre-dinner food choice.

Can I have a blublely?

_____

Tehila, asking for a small blue berry that grows on a bush.

EDUCATION

We learned three new Hebrew words today – pencil, scissors and book. I don't know how to say them in Hebrew, but those are the words we learned.

_____

Little Moshe (Segal) in kindergarten.

-How are you going to drive a car if you can't even look up a number in the phone book?
-*What's a phone book?*

_____

Aaron, in a generational disconnect.

A century ago, Andrea would have been a witch.

_____

Csaba, praising his wife's knowledge of the medicinal value of natural foods.

We lost, but we learned much more about the game.

_____

Ami, being philosophical about his soccer game.

I used to be indecisive. Now I don't know what to think.

_____

Dee, tergiversating.

The man who reads the Torah scroll at our synagogue service must have a speech impediment. I can't understand him at all. People say he's very good, but who can tell?

_____

Shoshana Neuer, doing a performance review.

ENVIRONMENT

There is so much glitter everywhere. Why do people leave glitter all over the ground instead of throwing it into a garbage can.

_____

Avi, to his mother, as they walked through the park.

EQUAL

-It's also my birthday today.
-Does that mean we're the same age?

_____

Yonatan, to his father, Noah.

EXERCISE

When I run a lot, I can feel my heart beeping.

_____

Yonatan, listening to himself.

-What were you boys playing downstairs?
-Hitting.

_____

Tova, questioning Michi.

-He started it!
-No! He hit me back first!

_____

Yehuda and Noah, shifting responsibilities.

At Marine Village, I am going to wear my fish-flops.

_____

Hannah, in anticipation.

I think I'll just lie here for a few minutes until my concussion goes away.

_____

Tat, after falling off his bike and banging his head on the pavement.

Mum, you brought very sweaty presents.

_____

Racheli, after running after balloons and balls.

I'll be in the gazebra.

_____

Levi, informing Naomi of his intended hiding place in the park.

EXCUSE

I don't know why I took your coat. I was already wearing mine.

———————————————

Jake Burak, after mistakenly taking Noah's raincoat.

You ran the red light. Don't you know how to read colours?

———————————————

Teenagers talking on the street as Tat bikes by.

EXILE

For the Passover holidays, I'm going back to my homeland.

———————————————

Yonatan, telling his teacher about Montreal where he was born.

Who put all those cigarette butts in the wall?

————————

Daveed, at the Western Wall in Jerusalem where people insert small pieces of paper with their prayers into the cracks.

EXISTENTIALISM

It's hard to live in a cup.

———————————————

Batya, explaining why her goldfish died.

From the back, everyone looks the same.

———————————————

Michi searching through a crowd.

F

FATIGUE

I haven't slept for twelve years.

Jewel, reflecting on raising six children.

FEAR

No monsters allowed in this room!

Jewel's sign on kids' room.

The Honk.

Eitan, talking about the superhero who turns green and muscular when angry.

FINANCE

Eitan: Mama, you spend a lot of money on food which leaves less to spend on Lego. I've stopped eating cookies so you can buy less food and more Lego.
Naomi: You're telling me this as you're eating a cookie. I see it in your hand.
Eitan: Fine, I'll start my diet next week.

Eitan, the budget genius

Do you get paid for playing baseball?
No.

So how do you make a living?

_____

Nava quizzing Michi the Baseball Pitcher.

FOOD

Do you want to eat now?
I can't sneeze and eat at the same time.

_____

Tat responding to Mum at Sneeze Number 4.

Eating lettuce is the same as brushing with toothpaste, because lettuce and toothpaste have the same ingredients.

_____

Dov the dental assistant.

Grits? That's cream of wheat with dirt in it.

_____

Tat, giving Ezra a culinary insight.

-What are you eating?
–Matza
-I thought matza came in balls.

_____

Naomi, in discussion with her Italian friend during Passover.

It was just lying around….so you should eat it.

_____

Auntie Marlene, proposing her muffins.

There's only one thing wrong with this cake...there's not enough of it.

_____

Tat, complimenting Genifer on her apple cake.

-What do monkeys like to bake?
-*Chocolate chimp cookies.*

An original joke by Eitan.

FRIENDS

Never sit next to the girl who brought fish sticks for lunch, after it was in her bag the whole day.

Talia, noting the effect of heat on food.

G

GEOGRAPHY

Mommy: It is so hot today.
Sammy: Why is it hot?
Mommy: Because we live in the Middle East.
Sammy: What? We live in the Middle East?!?

Tova, explaining geography to Sammy while out walking.

Why don't cities have middle names?

Tat's rhetorical question.

-How was your trip back home?
-*Like a long, deep massage on a warm sunny beach.*

Noah's description of the six-hour car ride home with three energetic kids in the back seat.

Yew Nork.

—————————————

Tehila's identification of the Big Apple.

GOURMET

Are there any spoiled eggs?

—————————————

Shua, wondering what's to eat.

GRAMMAR

What comes at the end of a sentence?

A pyramid.

—————————————

Levi on proper punctuation

GRANDPARENTING

Mazal tov to Jewel and Lazar on the birth of a new grandfather in Dallas.

—————————————

Synagogue announcer wishing congratulations to welcome Chedva and Ezra's new baby.

-You are very articulate. What 9-year old speaks that way?
-*Me!*

—————————————

Maayan, conversing with Tat.

My Grandpa which we call Tata is very tall just like his tall brother. They are kind of like Big Ben and the Empire State Building. His face reminds me of a perfect day to play outside. He has big blue eyes like the sky, a little bit of hair like a few small clouds. He has a short beard like the fresh smelling grass and best of all he has a big bright smile like the big warm sun. Usually when we see him he gives us a nice sweet candy that always makes us happy like we won the World Series. He could be as silly as a clown when he is with us but when he goes to work he can be as serious as a judge. When we have to say goodbye it breaks my heart like broken glass but when he gives us a goodbye hug it feels like a carpet is wrapped around me and that I am hugged by a bear.

Michi about Tat.

You ask if I'm tired? Do you think I look like this for nothing?

Margaret Aster, commenting on all the work she does for her children and grandchildren.

-Do you have any children at home?
-No, our children are your mother and her brothers and sisters.
-I mean little children.

Nava, on family relationships.

Can you put Vaseline on my lips?
-No, Vaseline is for boys.

Levi, refusing to share with Jewel for good reason.

H

HAPPY OCCASION

-Mum and Tat are only married forty years??
-*Let's see you be married for forty years.*

Maayan and Batya planning a party.

-You're adorable!
-*No, I am not Dora!*

Exchange between unknown shopper and Eitan at the store.

Good thing I have lips to cover my teeth.

Jewel, reflecting on oral hygiene.

A bar mitzvah is more important than a wedding. You only have one bar mitzvah, but you can get married many times.

Michi, on the realities of life.

-Where are you going?
-*To a wedding.*
-Are you marrying Ima? Will she be wearing her wedding dress?

Ayla, quizzing her father as her parents were leaving the house.

HEALTH

I have a stummy ache.

Levi's self-diagnosis.

For some reason, I have this irresistible urge to roll in the mud and eat garbage.

Dee, regaining consciousness after surgery to receive a porcine heart valve

I don't drink apple juice….No! Apple juice makes your teeth lellow.….I drink milk!….milk makes your teeth white!

Three year old Dov, nervously explaining dental hygiene to his dentist at his first visit.

I feel like a kangaroo. Everyone should have a pouch.

Jewel, enjoying the basket she affixed to her walker.

HELP

Spiders are your friends.

Tat, when asked by Naomi to get rid of an arachnoid.

-Just go up to the bullies and fart in their faces.
-But I don't have any more farts left after rest period.

Nava, commenting on her senior brother's tactical advice.

You're better than yoghurt.

Jewel to Lazar on his ability to induce sleep.

HOME

Lessons learned on moving day.

Lesson #1: When the dishwasher delivery guys tell you that they will show up any time from 7 AM to 7 PM, they'll be there at 7 PM.

Lesson #2: don't pack curry powder in a ziplock bag, even if it looks like magical fairy dust when it explodes. Especially if you don't know where the movers put the vacuum.

Naomi, fondly recalling her move to her new home.

-Is marijuana legal in New York?
-Not in our family.

Batya querying Yehuda.

HOUSE

I was going to ring your bell but you didn't have any front steps.

Naomi's neighbour during home renovations.

-Do you need any furniture for your new apartment?
-I could use a towel.

Gadiel Weigensberg, making do with less.

The only thing my room needs is room.

Gadiel Weigensberg, describing his living quarters.

Csaba? He's my brother from another mother.

_____

Naomi explaining the identity of a Sarna live-in guest.

Room service is here!

_____

Tova, upon receiving Mommy's tray of food while in quarantine during the pandemic.

I

IMPORTANT

I'm President of the Eruv Committee.

_____

Moshe, reminding others at Marine Village of his recent nomination.

I'm not a hairdresser: I'm really a dentist.

_____

Tova's Romanian hairdresser explaining his professional training while cutting her hair.

-I finally found my watch.
-*Where was it?*
-On my wrist. I don't know who put it there.

_____

Tat reveling in the discovery.

IMPOSSIBLE

It's hard to bark and swim at the same time.

_____

Jewel, watching a dog swim in Lake Champlain.

I'm not leaving until I win something.

Someone bemoaning his poor luck at a raffle.

My shadow is so annoying.

Hannah realizing it doesn't do what it's supposed to.

You can't read with your eyes closed.

Jewel, nodding off to dreamland.

INCLUSIVE

All our kids are here.

Tat, not noticing someone was missing.

Is everyone in Montreal called Sarna?

A lecturer from out of town, who coincidentally met or referenced several members of our family within one hour.

INCREDULOUS

-Can we buy a baby for me?
-*Babies come out of mommies' tummies.*
-Me too? You ate me up?

Little Ernest, figuring out where he came from.

The Earth is a magnet so nothing falls off of it.

Eddie, the astronomer.

-How many nipples does a boy have?
-Five nickels.

Nava, getting a response from Levi.

Is anything wrong? You look happy.

Overheard.

Last night I dreamt in Hebrew. It was great – I spoke without any mistakes at all.

Jewel, very pleased with herself.

Ex-smelly-armpits

Shua declaring the disarming wand charm in Harry Potter (expelliarmus).

INSIGHT

Nava: Men don't like to be wrong.
Csaba: That's because men are never wrong.
Nava: Men don't like to take advice.
Csaba: Because we have so much advice to give: so why take more.

A discussion without an end.

Auto-Correct finishes your sentences for you.

Like an annoying spouse.

Naomi, giving an IT description.

How much money did you spend on these groceries?
I don't know.
The border guard is going to ask.
All I know is that I saved $7.00.

Jewel answering the burning question of the day.

There's no logic to crazy.

Ezra's conclusion on trying to reason with some people.
It just slipped right out of me.

Tehila explaining why something suddenly dropped.

You know the word biography is pig latin.

Nava the etymologist.

J

JOY

Finally I found my own personal space.

Shua after wedging himself under the table between his father's feet.

JUSTICE

Hello Police, I want you to take my mother and father away.

Levi on the phone, taking legal recourse after Naomi tossed away his pacifier.

L

LANGUAGE

Doo-bill entendray.

Chedva explaining a phrase with a double meaning in Texas

Grammaire.

Naomi complaining French colleagues think she is talking about her grandmother or the Quebec town of Grand-Mère.

LIFE

No-one ever died from being healthy.

Ettie Saffran, answering, in any case "whatareyagonnado".

I am a shepherd of feelings.

Naomi, on her role as a parent and office worker.

I think I fell asleep on the toilet this morning.

Avi, seemingly refreshed

Mira to Oren: Why are you so tired?
Oren: Our grandson, the propeller, slept in my bed the whole night.

———————————

Oren, telling Mira, about their crazy-legs grandson, Yehuda.

Dead people live here.

———————————

The late Sam Lazarus, telling passengers as he drove by the cemetery.

We should go to more funerals together.

———————————

Jewel to Lazar, after one bereavement.

I'm not good at challenges. Reading is a challenge. So is reading from far away.

———————————

Nava on literacy.

You should go to a fancy barber to get rid of your old hair.

———————————

Levi offering Tat coiffure advice.

Jessy's succah must be well built because he's an engineer.
Yes, but he works at aerospace at Bombardier, so he wants to make sure it can fly.

———————————

Naomi and Tat discussing Jessy's succah building skills.

Can't change the lyrics without the permission of my former self.

———————————

Tat to Jewel on revising the words he sang on a recording from 1968 recently unearthed.

I enjoy everything that is served to me.

_____

Abigail quoting her mother on food she likes.

LAWYERS

"Notwithstanding the above provisions..."
-I'm not allowed to stand here?!?

_____

Naomi, reading a legal document to Eitan.

When you die, can I have all your jewelry...... especially the necklace you're wearing.

_____

Nava, staking a claim with Noami.

LIBERAL

My mother was very accepting of people, unless their sink was dirty.

_____

Bashi, on what parents teach kids.

LINGUISTICS

I spoke with the other children because I know how to speak Hebrew. I just said "Blah, blah blah"........to them.

_____

Talia, at the day care for the first time, immersed in a new language.

LITERARY

Shakespeare.
-*What is a Shakespeare?...Is Shakespeare a type of drink? I think I tasted it once.*

_____

Tova, reading bedtime stories.

-Is the bruise on your leg sensitive?
- *Yes, to literary criticism.*

_____

Lazar, responding to Jewel's concern after he fell off his bicycle.

LOST AND FOUND

-Ima, where did my treat go?
-*In your tummy.*
-I want it back now.

_____

Yonatan, mystified by the power of his stomach.

LOVE

-I love you, Mommy.
-*I love you too, Nava.*
-That's what I also tell my friend, Jakey, after we nap.

_____

Nava, telling Naomi about her true love at school.

-When you come home, I will give you lots and hugs and kisses.

-And hamburgers?

_____

Naomi and Eitan.

I love you, Eitan.
-You can't love me. You're not my mother.

_____

Eitan, discounting his grandmother's affection.

I felt love.

_____

Hannah reacting to baby Evan waving good-bye to her.

-Tell me about your day, Mamma.
-What do you not know about my day???? We've been together every minute for three weeks straight because of this pandemic. You know when I'm on the phone, what I eat, even when I go to the bathroom.…. What could there possibly be about my day that you don't know???? Now go to sleep!

_____

Nava and Naomi at bedtime.

Foods not to eat on the first date: corn on the cob, poppy seed cookies, spaghetti with sauce.

_____

Jewel and Lazar speculating.

I love you more now when you were twenty years old than I did when you were twenty.

_____

Jewel to Lazar, in a time warp, after listening to a long-lost recording of his songs.

I'm the best at not bragging about myself.

_____

Ami's self-appraisal

M

MARRIAGE

A woman without a husband is a spinster; and a man without a wife is a splinter.

_____

Batya, taking a wild guess.

You were the best-looking person at the cemetery.

_____

Tat to Mum after a funeral.

I can't marry Jakey. He never does what I tell him to do.

_____

Nava, talking about her classmate.

I was hit by another biker, head-on. I went flying and the bike is all twisted.
-Why didn't you call me right away?
I called all your numbers. No answer.
-I was shopping.

_____

Lazar, reporting to Jewel on his bike ride home from the office.

We're having a mop wedding at school. I'm the bride so I need a gown and a pail.

_____

Tehila's exciting day

MONARCHY

She looks pretty good for her age.

_____

Sammy, commenting on the Queen at the Royal Wedding.

Are the flower maids the children of the bride?

_____

Michi, watching a wedding ceremony.

-Naomi, I found the guest list for your wedding from ten years ago. Do you want it?
-No, I'm not planning to get married again anytime soon.

_____

Jewel, de-cluttering boxes in the basement.

MOTHER

I'm available to hold your baby. My arms are bored.

_____

Chedva to Naomi, who was holding baby Nava.

-Did you give your son and daughter-in-law your piano as a house-warming present?
-*No. We gave them the house as a house-warming present.*

_____

Lila Lowell with Jewel

MOTHER NATURE

The baby is sleeping in your tummy? Do you mean you have a crib in there too?

Little Gerald, when Marlene was pregnant.

MUSIC

You can never have too many trombones.

Josh Weigensberg, loaded down with Marie Josee's band instruments.

O

OPTIMIST

I don't want to hear any good news, unless it's about me.

Dov, upon being disturbed by an announcement.

I looked for the book everywhere.
-Did you look elsewhere?

Tat, seeking advice from Dov on a missing volume.

P

PARENTING

Without a Blackberry? How else can you bill time while rocking kids to sleep?!

Noah, dispensing legal advice at every opportunity.

What's your mother's name?
-Naomi, and her second name is Mamma

Levi, revealing family information.

Hi, Jewel. I called you Jewel.

Levi, mischievously acknowledging he called Mum by her first name.

My mother makes me do puzzles because I'm good at it.

Moshe, explaining his many activities.

All parents have to love their kids skinny or fat.

Tehila on family matters.

-Can we go to a movie?
-Okay.
Can we take another five kids?
-Okay.
-But please don't embarrass me.

Michi, worried about Tova's Hebrew accent and other things.

Nava, what would you like to do, just me and you?
-Go to Mum's house?

Jessy, looking for quality time with Nava.

I'm going to tell you something that will empower you: go get it yourself.

Yehuda, responding to Daveed who keeps asking for a glass of water.

Eddie: Morah Daniella is one more than Abba because she is 40 and he is 30.
Racheli: No that's 10 more than 30.
Eddie: Actually, she is 44…two fours.
Racheli: So she is 14 years older than Abba… I didn't realize Morah Daniella was in her 40's.

A mathematical dialogue.

No, Mommy too big….only Avi and only Eddie.

Avi, setting up the singing arrangement.

I'm not bossy. I'm just in charge.

Batya Zobin, explaining authority.

Aw, it's too bad you failed your driver's test.

Jewel and Lazar upon hearing the results from teenager Tova.

Where are you going?
-Out
I have an important question.
-What is it? I have to go.
How was your day?

Nava, trying to hold on to Mama

PARSIMONIOUS

When I buy a convertible car, I won't have to pay so much because it doesn't have a roof.

Sammy, contemplating a wise purchase.

PHILOSOPHY

-The font of ideas…
-You mean, fount?
-The Times Roman of ideas…

Yehuda, during a discourse at the table.

Now that will stay there forever.

Nava, after urinating in the snow.

Why did the man eat bread?
Because he had water in his ear.

Earliest recorded original riddle by Shirley Sarna.

PICNIC

Pick up the onion under the picnic table. We wouldn't want the skunk to have bad breath.

Jewel, worrying about animal welfare.

POLITICS

My right-wing friends are over-joyed with the election results. *As for the left-wings friends, I don't have any.*

Csaba, taking the public pulse after voting results.

PRAYER

Are you allowed to spell on the Sabbath?

Helen Liberman's legal question.

PRECAUTION

If I'm not careful, I might get Athlete's Face.

Jewel, massaging Sammy's feet after being cautioned by Tova.

I don't like leaving a gift for someone who makes more money than I do.

Asher Neudorfer contemplating leaving a Christmas tip for the postman.

PRECISION

I didn't hit her. I, um, clapped her, on the head.

Yonatan, when asked why Hannah, who was sitting next to him eating lunch, was crying.

-Don't go in. They're having a private conversation.
-*I won't disturb them: I just want to hear what they're saying.*

Eitan, clarifying his intent to Naomi.

Why is that man holding a paint brush to the Torah?

Hannah asking about the pointer.

Someone who is zealous is a zealot. Is someone who is jealous, a jeolot?

Shira Browns, visiting with her family.

PRIDE

Even if I were a piece of garbage, I wouldn't want to be thrown in the garbage.

Mayaan, lamenting over the discarding of a stale, store-bought chocolate cake.

-I've been wearing this shirt for four days.
-*You know, when your cousin, Asa, was fighting in the war this summer, he didn't change his socks or underwear for two weeks.*

-Wow, he's so lucky! My mother would never let me do that.

_____

Nine year old Michi and Jewel on the realities of dressing.

PROFILING

Walterstein

_____

Jessy, uttering what he thinks is a typical Ashkenazi family name.

Do you know Herb? You look exactly like Herb.
I mean, you wear the same shirt.

_____

Mentioned to Tat at a breakfast.

PUNCTUALITY

The class party will end approximately at 6 or 6:15 pm. Please pick up your child exactly on time.

_____

Note from Michi's teacher.

R

REALITY

She has the right to bare arms.

_____

Jewel, looking at photos of Batya wearing short sleeved tops.

-How many kids are in your class?

–All of them.

Yonatan, responding to Mum.

-Why don't you sit down and read a book?
–My body won't allow me.

Yonatan, actively discussing his physiology with Jewel.

RELIGION

You have to take a bath so that you will be clean.
–For Passover?

Nava, asking a relevant question.

This is the church Tat doesn't go to...and this is the other church he doesn't go to.

Jewel explaining a photo of Tat on his bike between two church spires.

Let me tell you how I went from being a camp counselor to Chief Rabbi of the United Arab Emirates.

Yehuda, addressing summer camp alumni.

S

SAD

Now he's saying kat-dish.

Gerald, on hearing about someone mourning his deceased feline.

SARCASM

That's like putting lingerie on a monkey.

Dee, commenting on his friend's plan to renovate his house located in a bad neighbourhood.

SCIENCE

How do they make recycled paint? Do they peel it off the walls?

Jewel, asking a hardware question.

Abba, does everyone know that you have a lot of hair on your body? Should I tell them?

Avi, making a physiological discovery.

A tape measure has two measurements: cinnamon and Fahrenheit

Nava, very seriously and with authority, explaining to Naomi the measurements on a tape measure.

I didn't know fake chicken was a real thing.

Levi amazed at a soup mix package.

Its bark is bigger than it.

Lazar, startled by a shrimpy dog

Who made the floor so low?

_____

Lazar, refusing to bend to pick something up.

Nobody from here is from here.

_____

Mum, after realizing the Houston synagogue is in the Twilight Zone.

Levi, how much is a meter?
About an inch.

_____

Levi being quizzed by Michael Saar.

Ezra: I'm allergic to fish.
Sephardi host mother: It's okay. It's spicey.

_____

Serving advice from a motherly chef.

Is a sugar rush in a hurry?

_____

Yehuda Kessler quizzing his parents

How did Nalli become so cute?
Cute grandparents.

_____

Avi seeking Tat's response.

Nava: Papa, did you know that you can't even brush your teeth on Yom Kippur?
Jessy: Yes, because on Yom Kippur, we imitate the angels.
Nava: Those angels sure must have a lot of cavities!

_____

A dental theology dialogue: Naomi adding, Angels don't even have teeth!

SECRET

Naomi: ....Now enter your password.
Mummy: Password?...*my* password?!? (*blank stare*).
Naomi: Ya, password. Yours.
Mummy: I don't know....what is it?
Naomi: I'm not telling you.
Mummy: Why not? It's *my* password!

―――――――――――

Naomi, helping Mum log on to Facebook.

SENSITIVE

I am a sweat-detector.

―――――――――――

Moshe, after sitting on the shoulders of a student dancing and hopping.

I will pray for you.

―――――――――――

Eitan to Ami, after he accidentally broke the light fixture in the basement where they were throwing balls.

I didn't trade, I switched.

―――――――――――

Avi explaining the fate of his school lunch.

SIGHT

Don't worry. I have X-ray vision. I saw through the bus.

―――――――――――

Tova, anticipating a pedestrian darting out from behind another vehicle as she was driving.

SPACE

I don't want to be here. I don't want to be there. I don't want to be anywhere.

_____

Dee, finding no place for himself.

SPEAKING

Whenever I want to say hospital, for some reason I say airport.

_____

Chedva, according to Ezra.

It is not nice to talk Russian hora.

_____

Yonatan, explaining the rules of slander.

SPIES

Under-covered.

_____

Moshe, describing a secret world.

SPORTS

First, let me see you run.

_____

Dee to Jewel, in her 9ᵗʰ month of pregnancy when she invited him to play tennis with her.

I'm afraid I'm going to drain.

———————————————

Eddie to Chedva, on why he doesn't want to go swimming.

Consider it sports equipment.

———————————————

Tova, consoling Jewel over having to temporarily use a walker.

Now I know the meaning of aqua-torture.

—————————

Jewel's swimming buddy after a strenuous exercise class.

Your left hiking stick is shorter than the right stick.
Does this mean the stick inspector will give me a ticket?

—————————

Jewel and Lazar out for a hike with their poles.

SUMMER

What are you doing?
–Nothing.

———————————————

Michi, methodically pounding the sand on the beach with a rock in a minnow net.

SUMMERTIME

I like Marine Livage.

—————————

Daveed, in the country by the lake.

Frozed out.

Tehila, on the effect of a cold winter.

SUPERPHARM

Where are all the animals?

Michi, looking around the drugstore.

SURPRISE

Maayan, brace yourself!

Batya to Maayan, when Tova was about to give her a present of new clothes. This was after Tova gave Moshe turquoise socks with glitter.

Why did I wake up covered in smiley-face stickers this morning?

Tova, after Ilan decorated her pajamas while she slept.

-I wanted to see if my underwear came alive in the dark.

-Ezra, explaining why he slowly closed the bureau drawer on his lower lip.

Wake me up when my birthday surprise gets here.

Tat, on preparing for the surprise that wasn't.

-Nothing in that washroom works.
-Maybe it's an exhibit.

Tova, explaining the Museum to Tat.

T

TASTE

My favourite food is...ice!

_____

Michi, the gourmet.

One part of my brain is wondering why I don't open my chips. A second part is saying it's because I am not finished my drink. A third part is wondering if I should eat them at the same time.

_____

Racheli, in a quandry.

TASTIER

My favourite vegetable is cow.

_____

Noah, considering the food options.

TASTIEST

Could you ask mommy and daddy if they could also buy me a cloud?

_____

Ilan to Talia at the park, when he saw a boy eating cotton candy.

TEEN ANGST UPON A SPRAINED ANKLE

I'm hungry.
Stop talking to me.
Help me walk, don't touch me.

Grunt.
I'm hungry again.

Mommy!
Do sprained ankles cause farts?

I'm not going to school.
Tell me why I should ice my ankle but don't give me a speech.

Why do I need crutches?
Can I wear a sock? I don't want my friends to see my toes.

———————————————

Michi, the perfect patient

I injured my knee by sitting too long.

———————————

Tova's self-diagnosis

THIRSTY

-What are you putting in your coffee?
-*Amaretto. I use it instead of sugar. Mmm. It needs more sugar.*

———————————

Jewel, tasting her drink.

This baby has surplus spit.

———————————————

Batya, holding a young sibling

TIME

When were you born?

−1950
Is that in the 80's?

Moshe, cross-examining Jewel on her birthday.

When it's night, every hour is dark o'clock.

Tat, commenting on winter.

In the olden times, you would have to send a text in an envelope.

Eitan, thinking back.

Client by email: When can we talk? Is Now a good time?
Lazar: Yes. Just call.
Client calling one hour later: Is it still Now?

Lazar and his nervous client

When do your teenagers get up?
At the crack of noon.
What time is it?
The morning of the afternoon.

Tova reporting her conversation with a neighbour

TIMING

It looks like Mommy started a very, very important phone call. I better whine and take a fit.

Ilan thinking, as Tova takes the call

It doesn't matter if I help Mum. She's going to win anyway.

_____

Daveed, the card master

TIRED

You're asleep.
-No, I'm listening.

_____

Jewel, in denial

TRUST

Give me all your money. I'll invest it for you.

_____

Moshe, age 11, advising Daveed, age 8.

Just because a story didn't happen doesn't mean it's not true.

_____

Said by a bible scholar.

U

ULTIMATUM

Unless you get into the car right now, you'll have to stay with Mum and go to a funeral and a gynecologist appointment with her.

_____

Tova, presenting choices to Sammy.

UNDERSTAND

I'm trying to make magic, but it's not working.

Ilan, after trying to make a small toy disappear under a napkin and repeating abracadabra several times.

Who created Starbucks?

Racheli contemplating.

I know Swedish from reading the IKEA furniture catalogue.

Aaron Koller telling Tat about his new vocabulary.

UNITY

We're your family away from family away from your family.

Naomi to Csaba.

W

WANT

You're not really hungry: you're thirsty.

Tat, to kids asking for ice cream.

You're not really thirsty: you're tired.

Jewel, to kids asking for a drink at bedtime.

WARNING

-Mommy, there's a fly in the car.
-Does it have its seat-belt on?

Sammy and Tova having a driving discussion.

The arctic is cold because it's cold in outer space.

Shua, the weatherman.

WEDDINGS

We'll be wearing our best software.

Tat, lamenting non-attendance at Talia's wedding, except by Zoom.

WIT

"I've always felt concerned about my need to give advice," one attendee said. "The first meeting was great, though if you ask me, they should have done it a little differently."

Yehuda, from his article on compulsive givers of advice.

WORK

-You should get a job fixing bicycles.
-Where would I get one?
-You could be our personal bicycle fixer.

Neighbour's eight-year old, as Tat repaired her flat tire.

When I grow up, I'm going to buy a saw.

Eitan, watching Tat cut wood in the back yard.

I want to cut down the bushes. Can I have the tweezers?

Eitan, the gardener.

Y

YEP

The best way to get rid of a bee is to spray starch it.

Ezra, continuing a family tradition.

YOUNG

-Is that a new baby?
-Yes, it's still under warranty.

Jessy, commenting on a new family member.

YOUNGER

There was an old lady like you….. but you're not old.

Batya, telling Jewel an engrossing story.

TOVA THE DOG DETECTIVE

t started out as a normal day for fourteen year old Michi.

On his way to school, he passed a man walking his dog on the pathway. All of a sudden, the unpredictable happened. Unprovoked, the dog lunged toward Michi and bit him on his calf. Ouch! Yet, the owner took his dog and walked away.

Michi continued to school, limping and in pain. He called home to relate the incident. His parents were concerned about rabies, so his father, Gerald, took him to the local medical clinic. The doctor said they must find the dog within twenty-four hours to determine whether the dog had received its rabies shots. If they couldn't find the dog, Michi would have to undergo a long series of painful injections against rabies. But Michi had never seen the dog or his owner before! The dog had to be found.

Everyone in the family began scouring the neighborhood looking for the dog. His mother, Tova, decided to become a detective to find the culprit. The next day at the same time, she went to the path where the incident had occurred. She waited in her car disguised in-con-spic-uously, taking photos of people walking their dogs and texting the photos to Michi, "Is this the dog? Is this the dog?" No luck!

Tova did not know that while she was watching the path, she was being watched by a local undercover policeman who thought she was acting suspiciously. Why was she wearing a large brimmed sun hat and sunglasses? Why was she parked in the same spot for so long taking photos? Did she have a gun in her large handbag? He cautiously approached and asked for her citizenship papers and other identification. The policeman asked her many questions. Tova explained nervously why she was there. The policeman accepted what he thought was a strange story. He asked her to move on and warned her not to do anything illegal.

Tova soon spotted the bad owner and his dog! She confronted him, saying "I have been waiting for you for two hours. You and your biting dog are in big trouble."

The owner said the dog, whose name was Chess, had received its rabies shot. Yet neither the owner nor the dog bothered to apologize. Tova alerted the city veterinarian whose friends in the law enforcement department took special "care" of the owner. That means, he was given a big ticket. They also took away his dog for observation for ten days [bad dog].

Michi recovered well from the incident and thanked his mother for saving him from having to get painful injections against rabies for a month. He continues to walk along the same path to school, a little bit wiser.

The End (woof)

EITAN GROWS

Seven year old Eitan is growing so quickly! He is taller than everyone else in his class or the older class or the even older class. He is even taller than his Grade One teacher! Some people, when they see him, think he's in high school.

As he gets bigger and l-o-n-g-e-r, his bed seems to be getting narrower and shorter. Eitan sleeps in the lower bed of a bunk bed. His feet and head almost touch the ends of the bed. What will his parents do when Eitan outgrows his bed? Where will Eitan sleep?

1. Should Eitan sleep on the floor or.... on the stairs? Not very comfortable.
2. Maybe Eitan should learn to sleep on his hands and knees? Not very possible.
3. Or Eitan can stay awake for the next ten years until he goes to university. Impossible!
4. Should Eitan sleep outside in a tent?
5. Or under a ping pong table in the gym or on a park bench? Under the dining room table? In the bathtub? On the roof? In the car?

One day Eitan will need an extra-long double sized bed. None of the rooms in the house are large enough for that sized bed. That's why his parents are thinking of building an extension to the house. This will cost a lot of money.

All because Eitan is outgrowing his bed!

6. Maybe Eitan should sleep in the basement?
7. Should his parents convert the garage into a bedroom for Eitan? Mama and Papa will have to park their two cars in the driveway. Eitan would have to shovel the snow off the cars before he goes to school in the morning. (He won't like that!)
8. Maybe he should sleep in a trailer, in a shipping container, or in a dump truck in the backyard.
9. Maybe Eitan should sleep at his grandparents' house? Or get his own apartment?
10. Maybe his parents should buy a bigger house! That also would cost a lot of money.

All because Eitan is outgrowing his bed!

Another idea is to take the money that would have gone into building an extension or buying a bigger house; and move the whole family to Israel. However the apartments in Israel are small, the bedrooms are small and the beds are narrow and short. Mama and Papa will have to find new jobs, buy an apartment and a new car (which would also be smaller). Eitan, Nava and Levi will go to a new school and speak in Hebrew. However, they will be so happy to be living in Israel that they won't mind any of this.

All because Eitan is outgrowing his bed!

PART TWO:

REAL WORDS ON THEIR OWN

C hildren are notorious users of words. Their grasp of the word is often as tenuous as a grasp of a wet and wiggling fish.

We have collected words for this dictionary which best typify the ability of children to confidently or seriously or light-heartedly speak in a language that has been thrust upon them.

Let us remember though, that language is only one of several means of expression: a child would prefer to scream, kick or smile if his or her needs would more readily be satisfied. The very use of the listed words indicates the child's preference for language as a means of communication. The malformation or contortion which the word suffers indicates the incomplete grasp, or in another sense, the excessive expectation the child brings to the force and effect of diction.

We have chosen words which, although twisted in meaning, do for the most part have a true existence and significance in the English language. As may be noted, a few are cunning, many disarming, all innocent.

A

ABORT   on deck, as in "all abort". The train conductor calls "All Aboard."

ACE OF SPACE   a playing card. A powerful one to have in any card game.

AIR COMMISSIONER   air cooling device. A very valuable machine to have in hot weather.

AIR PAIN   an air vehicle. How does an airplane that weighs so much fly through the air?

AISLE   a river in Egypt. A natural source of irrigation and hydro power.

ALL WHITE   all is right. A pre-condition to being happy is to recognize everything is in its best place.

AMMONIA   a medical condition. Pneumonia is a dreaded disease that usually requires a trip to the hospital.

AND   a black insect; also, the end of an arm. The industrious ant teaches us many things, even if it does not have a hand.

ARROW   sixty minutes. A watch only shows one hour at a time.

ASH	trash. Trash becomes garbage when it is not usable.

B

BANK IT	a warm cover. A blanket not only warms, it comforts.
BEARD	an adult beverage. Beer is not a drink for children.
BEREAVE	breathe. We have to open our mouths and noses to take in air.
BIRD	a spontaneous expulsion of gas from the mouth. You can't help making this noise to clear your stomach.
BLASTER	white powder used to cover wall cracks. Somehow, the plaster sticks to the wall in a flat way.
BREAST	air inhaled, as in "a breast of fresh air". The reason for breathing.
BROWN	to die in water. There is no colour in drowning, only sorrow.
BURT	a flying fowl. How do birds rise up and come down so gracefully?

C

CAD a feline. Many people think cats are lazy but smart.

CAKE a mantle worn by a mythical hero. A cape does not have any. pockets: so, what good does it do?

CAMEL BREAD bread with kimmel seeds. Many people like it toasted in a sandwich.

CAPE a dessert made of flour, often with icing. The problem is that the icing is usually better than the cake it covers.

CEMENT lower floor of a house. Downstairs can be cold, damp, dark, spooky, but always quiet.

CHECK MAID a chess move. The only way to win the game: by taking the king.

CHEW clothing for the foot. It is important that shoes match and are worn on the appropriate feet.

CHICKEN a room used for food preparation. Sometimes, the whole family hangs out in the kitchen.

CHIT MONK	squirrel's relative. The chipmunk is smaller and cuter than its larger cousin.
CHOP SEWER	a Chinese food. Some people don't like such a salty dish.
CHOPPING	searching through stores for purchases. Sometimes it can take hours if you don't know what you are looking for.

D

DART	black. The night is always black outside, but hopefully not inside.
DENTAL FLUFF	a string used to clean between teeth. A toothbrush is not enough.
DIPPER	a mechanical device used for zipping. The inventor of this item is a hero, except when it breaks.
DUMMY	where food goes. It probably looks like a big plastic bag.
DRAIN	a body organ used for thinking. Some people have big ones, making them smarter.

E

EAST   leavening agent. What a magical way to make bread.

F

FATS OF LIFE   reality. What is true is what is real, most of the time.

FERSTER   a university teacher. This is an occupation many aspire to, because of the respect students give.

FING   an object. What is tangible could also be intangible.

FIRSTY   a sensation requiring the drinking of liquid. It does not matter what you drink, as long as it contains lots of water.

FLUTE   a viral infection causing fever. Being sick is no fun, even with all the attention you get.

G

GLUBS   hand warmers. Certain people love mittens while others favour fingered gloves.

GRAPES	mechanical device for slowing cars, as in "step on the grapes!" It is not good practice to drive with one foot on the gas and the other on the brake.
GRILL	a young female. There is no male equivalent.
GROW	a black bird. They can be very scary when they land in flocks and make their caw-ing noise.

H

HAND CUPS	police restraining device. It is next to impossible to get out of hand-cuffs or do anything with your arms.
HARD	an organ in the chest. It beats like a drum, always with the same rhythm.
HEARSE	four legged animal. A horse is a strong and faithful animal because it never complains.
HOLD	a perforation. The wonderful thing about a hole is that both sides of it are the same.
HOT	to jump on one foot. We actually move faster by hopping like a kangaroo.

HUM BREE	a feeling only food can satisfy. There are favourite foods, and then items that just fill up a stomach without much taste.

I

IMPARTMENT	important. Important is not necessarily like urgent: more like first things first.
I RAN	A metal. It's strange that some foods contain iron, and that it is healthy to eat.

J

JELLY	happy ("for he's a jelly good fellow"). Being happy makes others happy as well.

K

KOOL	a place populated by students. Teachers take the place of parents for most of the day.
KOVERED	cupboard. The only place to safely store fragile dishes.
KRACK	sound made by a duck. It's strange that every sound for every occasion is a quack.

L

LIE BERRY a place of books. No talking, no food, no wrestling, just reading.

LOST IN FOUNTAIN where lost clothes and articles are kept. You get some of the best stuff in the Lost and Found.

M

MARVEL a round glass ball. The more marbles, the more they look like a cache of diamonds.

MAT angry. Losing control is another excuse for being mad.

MIKER WAVE an oven. A magic box that warms up things but doesn't get hot.

MOP a flying insect. Moths used to eat clothes and make holes. That stopped once moth balls were invented, and polyester took over from wool.

MOP OILY a board game. Even small children now understand the economics of monopoly.

MR. FISH troublesome. Both kids and adults share this trait.

MUST STAFF	growth of hair on the upper lip. Some men like to wax it, curl it or simply shave it off.

N

NAPPLE	a popular fruit. You can make sauce or apple cake with it.
NEOPLOLITICS	three-flavoured ice cream with layers of chocolate, vanilla and strawberry.
NO	white frozen rain. Snow can be fluffy or icey.

O

OFFER	a person who writes books. Authors like to hear from their readers.
OVERFLOATING	when water goes over the edge as in "The toilet is overfloating!" What a wonder this is, especially when it drowns the floor.

P

PAINED	oil-based or latex colouring liquid. Everything looks new when it is freshly painted.
PEAS	please. A polite introduction to a request.

PETARD	a six or twelve-stringed musical instrument. Many folk singers entertain using a guitar in an emotional way.
PIG	a dried sweet fruit. The difference between a dried and fresh fig is astounding.
POLO BEAR	a white arctic animal. What a majestic animal, covered in an all-white coat.
POND	chess piece. The pawn is an expendable member of the team but not really.
POSED	a short pillar often supporting a fence. Good fences and posts make good neighbours.
POST CARD	marine police patrol. They go up and down the coast looking to help stranded boaters.

R

RAISIN	a black bird. It's hard to tell the difference between a crow and a raven.
REEL	a round rubber object rotating on an axle. A reel is a reel.
RIGHT	a state of maturity of fruit. Fruit can be very delicate, soft, hard, juicy or wrinkled.

ROAST CAKE   a skate with wheels. Roller derbies are the best places to use roller skates.

RUDE   subterranean part of a tree. Most roots dive very deeply into the ground.

S

SCREAM   used in movie projection. The anticipation of seeing the show on the screen is always tremendous.

SEA-BELL   a safety restraining device in a car. It may be uncomfortable, but the seat-belt is the best protection in the event of a sudden stop.

SEEP   to lie dormant. Sleeping and dreaming go together. Nightmares disturb sleep.

SHARK   reaction to an electric current. Never stick anything into the electric outlet, especially metal, or you might get a shock.

SHAVE   sunless spot (the shave of a tree). The temperature is cooler in the shadow of tree leaves.

SHEEP   a linen mattress covering. We change our sheets every so often.

SICK CAR	a tobacco product. The smelliest smoke comes from the cigar.
SINGING HEATERS	radio speakers in a car. Sometimes the amplifiers don't work well enough.
SIP	a crunchy potato snack. Usually too salty or oily and goes with any meal.
SMOKES MEAT	a delicatessen meat. It is best in a sandwich with pickles and mustard.
SNIPPERS	casual shoes. Never walk bare-foot in the house.
STY	the heavens. The sky is home to the sun, clouds and stars.
SUPPER AID	spread apart. Either we are together or separate.

T

TAMBOURINE	orange citrus fruit. The tangerine is the smaller sister of the orange and the grapefruit.
THUMB TAG	tack for pressing with the thumb. The better fastener is magnetic.
TIE YARD	fatigued. Whether you exercise or sit still, you can always feel tired.

TOILET TREES	cosmetics and stuff. Perfumes and creams make the day.
TOMATO SOCKS	substance poured on spaghetti. It is hard to make a good first impression by eating this dish, even though it is delicious.
TOOTH TAPE	tooth cleaner. Brushing is always a chore, but an essential one for healthy teeth.
TUFFS	tusks. Elephants use their tusks to fight and to protect.
TURBAN TIME	a paint solvent. It may smell strong, but turpentine does the job.

U

UNDER A WRIST	taken into custody by police officer - "You're under arrest."
UNIFIER	humidifier. Breathing is much easier in a slightly humid environment.
UNIVERSE	female reproductive organ. Babies are not born from the stomach.
URF	the contents of ground. There is a difference between earth and dirt.

V

VARVA-QUE   outdoor roasting apparatus. Barbacue is mostly ash and fire.

VIRUS   a flower. The elegance and scent of the iris is unbeatable.

W

WALNUT   book shelves in a unit. A bookcase filled with reading material warms a room.

WANE   precipitation. People usually can't find their umbrellas when they need them.

WELT   a pit in the ground with water at the bottom. Make sure the bucket doesn't have a hole.

WHIFF   a preposition denoting accompaniment. Being with is usually better than being without.

WINK   flying limb of a bird. This is why we can't fly using our arms.

WOES   a prized flower. Red roses are a favorite, even if they don't have a perfume about them.

WOOL	the planet. The world is either round or oval.

Y

YEARS	auditory organs in the head. Usually they hear; often, not.
YEH-WHOA	a light colour. Yellow is a cousin of green, red and orange.

www.ingramcontent.com/pod-product-compliance
Lightning Source LLC
Chambersburg PA
CBHW031225120626
46545CB00003B/996